ATTITUDES TOWARD HANDICAPPED PERSONS

A STUDY OF THE DIFFERENTIAL EFFECTS OF FIVE VARIABLES

by

Franklin F. Saunders

Doctor of Philosophy

A Dissertation

THE FLORIDA STATE UNIVERSITY

COLLEGE OF EDUCATION

1969

Reprinted in 1975 by

R AND E RESEARCH ASSOCIATES
4843 Mission Street, San Francisco 94112
18581 McFarland Avenue, Saratoga, California 95070

Publishers and Distributors of Ethnic Studies
Editor: Adam S. Eterovich
Publisher: Robert D. Reed

Library of Congress Card Catalog Number

74-29579

ISBN

0-88247-323-9

ACKNOWLEDGEMENTS

The writer expresses gratitude to Dr. James G. Foshee, Major Professor and Chairman; Dr. Ronald C. MacKinnon who acted in the capacity of dissertation director; Dr. Ralph L. Witherspoon, Mrs. Ellen A. Thiel, Dr. Nancy J. Douglas, and Dr. Jack G. May, the members of the doctoral committee, who, both individually and as a group, provided valuable help in directing this study.

A special note of appreciation is offered to Dr. John D. Webster, Dr. Howard W. Stoker, Miss Betty A. Haddock, Mrs. Barbara A. Dilbert, Mrs. Meryl R. Warren, Mrs. Regina Caveny, Dr. F. J. King and Dr. Gerald J. Schluck.

The Human Resources Center, Albertson, New York, provided useful information, reference materials and the measuring instrument.

The study is dedicated to my daughter, Sharon, whose encouragement has been a constant source of support.

Above all else, I thank God.

F.F.S.

TABLE OF CONTENTS

LIST OF TABLES

I. INTRODUCTION

Historically, attitudes became a focal problem in experimental research about the first decade of this century. Thurstone (1929) attributed to Cattel the pioneer work in the meansurement of social values, but Thurstone and Thorndike (1935) must be considered as among those pioneers who attempted to develop scientific attitude assessment instruments. Thurstone observed that the study of attitudes suffered from the serious handicap that the phenomena (attitudes) were exceedingly difficult to describe in objective terms, to say nothing of quantitative measurement. In 1935 Allport wrote that the concept of attitude was probably the most distinctive and indispensable concept in contemporary American social psychology. A volume summarizing the state of social psychology in 1937 emphasized the point that perhaps no single concept within the whole realm of social psychology occupied a more nearly central position than that of attitudes (Murphy, Murphy, & Newcomb, 1937). The study of attitudes has not been solely the concern of the psychologists; educators, sociologists, and anthropologists have also focused their investigative attentions on the problem (Sherif & Cantril, 1947).

Attitudes may be defined as predispositions to respond in a particular way toward specific subjects (Rosenberg and Hovland, 1960). Being predispositions, they are not directly observable nor can they be measured except by inference. Attitudes are inferred from the way one responds to particular stimuli. Saying that a man has an unfavorable attitude toward the handicapped elicits the expectancy that he will perceive their actions with negative feelings and will tend to avoid the handicapped. Attitudes are inferred after noting two factors which are observable, (1) the evoking stimuli and (2) the various types of responses. The measurement of the latter is basic to the analysis of differences and changes in attitude.

A theory of attitude measurement must be based on the assumption that the subject's attitudes may be measured by his expression of acceptance or rejection of opinions; and that the subject's expressions may be quantified and weighted (Thurstone & Chave, 1929). A second assumption is that the attitude assessor is used in situations in which one may reasonably expect people to tell the truth about their convictions and opinions. The theory of attitude measurement is concerned with locating individuals along an attitude continuum on the basis of the opinions that they accept or reject.

It is only in the past ten years that measuring instruments have been developed with reliability and validity adequate for the task of assessing attitudes toward disabled persons generally, rather than toward specific disability groups; i.e., blind, mentally ill, etc. Few research studies have investigated attitudes toward disabled persons, and the studies which have been done in this area are equivocal.

Some questions for which answers were sought in the present study are: Do college students have favorable or unfavorable attitudes toward disabled persons? Can attitudes toward disabled persons be changed by an introductory course in special education? Are variables such as course orientation, college major, grade level, sex, and age significantly associated with attitudes toward disabled persons?

Limitations of Attitude Measurement

The success achieved in the past ten years in the field of the measurement of attitudes may be regarded as a major accomplishment. The rate of progress is so great that further achievement seems inevitable; but, there arc inherent limitations in all methods of testing. Measurement can deal mainly with attitudes that are common. In forcing attitudes into a scale some restructuring is done to the thought process. Attitude scales should be regarded only as the roughest approximation of the way in which attitudes actually exist in the personality of individuals.

Rationalization and deception inevitably occur, especially when the attitudes studied pertain to moral or social values. Lack of insight, ignorance, suspicion, fear, guilt, undue enthusiasm, or even a knowledge of the investigator's purpose may invalidate an inquiry. Tests developers must take these factors into account.

Each person possesses many contradictory attitudes, and his mental set at the moment of submitting to a scale may tell only a part of the story. Furthermore, attitudes often change, and an investigation made under one set of conditions may not for long present a true pictue of the attitudes of any given group. There is, consequently, a need for further and continuing study.

3

II. PROBLEMS

Are there significant differences in attitudes toward the disabled between those students who choose people oriented courses of study when compared with students in more technically oriented courses? Is course selection a significant factor in attitudes toward those who are handicapped? Does an introductory course in special education result in different attitudes toward persons with disabilities?

Purpose

The purpose of the study was to investigate three areas. First, are the attitudes of college students who choose education courses significantly different from other college students whose major fields are more technically oriented; i.e., engineering, mathematics, and business? Second, will there be a change of attitude following exposure to a course in special education? Third, are the variables of academic major, grade, age, and sex related to differences in attitudes toward the disabled?

Hypotheses

1. The mean of the Attitude Toward Disabled Persons (ATDP) pretest scores of groups choosing to take an introductory course in special education will be equal to the mean of the ATDP posttest scores of the same groups following exposure to an

4

introductory course in special education.

2. The means of the ATDP pretest scores of groups choosing to take an introductory course in special education will be equal to the means of the ATDP pretest scores of other groups in engineering, business, mathematics, and elementary education.

3. The means of the ATDP pretest scores of groups choosing people oriented courses (special education and elementary education) will be equal to the means of the ATDP pretest scores of groups choosing more technically oriented courses (engineering, business, and mathematics).

4. The mean of the ATDP pretest scores of each group not exposed to the introductory course in special education will be equal to the mean of the group's ATDP posttest scores.

5. The mean of the combined ATDP pretest scores of all females from all eight groups will be equal to the mean of the combined ATDP pretest scores of all males from all groups.

6. The means of the combined ATDP pretest scores of all groups at each age level will be equal.

7. The means of the combined ATDP pretest scores of all groups at each grade level (sophomores, juniors, seniors, and graduate students) will be equal.

III. REVIEW OF THE LITERATURE

The review of the literature is in two parts, one on instrument development and one on attitude studies. The instrument development section begins with an outline of the development of attitude measuring instruments together with a discussion of strengths and weaknesses in attitude measurement. Comparisons are then made with the instrument used in the present study. The review is focused upon instrument development which makes attitude measurement possible, and upon those attitude studies which relate generally to the assessment of attitudes toward disabled persons. The illustrations used to show instrument development are selected for relevance and contrast to the present study.

Instrument Development

A review of the literature shows instrument development to be a major concern of attitude studies about handicapped persons. Because of the critical importance of a good instrument in attitudes investigation, the review will emphasize the growth of measuring scales which are fundamental to current research efforts. A second reason for emphasis on attitude measurement is that it serves as a useful means of reviewing attitude studies in a sequential, organized manner.

It is only in the past 30 years that instruments measuring attitudes toward disabilities have received much attention. The early instruments lacked sophistication and frequently presented no evidence of reliability or validity (Yuker, Block, & Young, 1966). Some instruments may be classified as scorable and others as non-scorable. Instruments also differ in whether they attempt to measure attitudes toward the disabled in general. The instruments oriented toward disabilities in general are a very recent development (Yuker, et al., 1966).

An inspection of the literature indicates that studies of attitude measurement may be organized into four general categories; i.e., non-scored instruments (of which there are two kinds, unstructured and structured), simple scored instruments, attitudes scales, and other specialized scorable techniques. The use of each will be illustrated together with examples and comments relevant to the present study.

Non-Scored Instruments

Unstructured. The simplest method of assessing attitudes is the unstructured questionnaire or interview. In such measures the S is asked direct questions about his attitudes toward a disability or disabled persons. The unstructured questionnaire method was used as early as 1933 by Koehler in a study of the attitudes of university instructors toward blind students. It is still used in many attitudes surveys, particularly those of employer attitudes toward disabled workers (Jennings, 1961; Barton, Colardarci, & Carlson, 1954; Reeder, 1958; Garrett, 1964). Usually the data from unstructured questionnaires are treated only in terms of frequency of response for each item. The studies of Jennings (1961) yield a pattern of specific types of attitudes toward disability, but do not give measures that permit inferential

7

statistical analysis of overall attitudes toward disability.

On the basis of a non-scored instrument, Jennings (1951) reported the results of interviews with 20 employers. She found that employer attitudes reflected a lack of confidence in the ability of disabled persons, a tendency toward exaggerated sympathy, an inability to accept the handicapped as a member of the so-called normal staff, and an erroneous concept of the handicapped person's rate of absenteeism.

Structured. The simplest of the non-scorable structured schedules are the 2-point response categories of "yes-no," "true-false," or "agree-disagree." The responses are made to direct questiosn similar to those in the earlier interviews but with the interviewer removed. Baskin and Herman (1961) attempted to measure attitudes of both rehabilitation and non-rehabilitation students toward persons with cerebral palsy. They used 12 statements about cerebral palsy such as: "It is embarrassing to be seen with a cerebral palsy person in public," and "Many cerebral palsys have higher intelligence than normal people." Subjects were required to answer yes and no to each item. The investigators (Baskin & Herman, 1951) made no attempt to scale the items but instead listed each item separately as favorable or unfavorable. No scoring was attempted. The questionnaire was favorable if most of the responses were favorable, and unfavorable if most responses were unfavorable. The results indicated that females were more favorable than males, and those who had more contact with the cerebral palsied were more favorable. However, recent studies have left both of these

8

findings open to question (Yuker, et al., 1966). It appears that better instruments and improved experimental design may obtain results which tend to refute earlier findings. The structured non-scorable two category scales are inadequate for statistical analysis and the assessment of attitudes.

In contrast to the two category scales of Baskin and Herman, Strong (1931) used three response categories (liking, disliking, and indifferent) in a study of comparative attitudes toward dissimilar persons. Strong, who was the first to study comparative attitudes toward unlike groups, used classifications such as "cripples," "blind people," "deaf mutes," "negroes," "conservatives," "aged," and "athletes." Both Maglione (1965) and Strong (1931) reported more favorable attitudes toward the blind than toward the deaf. Other comparisons were made, but the statistical significance of the results of Strong's studies were not reported. Blanton and Nunnally (1964), on the other hand, reported that adolescents rated deaf persons higher, but that the differences were not statistically significant.

The studies all used non-scorable instruments. The instruments do not lend themselves to inferential statistics. Non-scorable instruments use a nominal scale which is limited even when compared with the ordinal scale which will be considered next.

Ranking Procedures. The most sophisticated of the non-scored instruments are the ranking procedures which are used to elicit preferences among professionals or employers for working with various types of handicapped persons such as the hearing disabled, the emotionally disturbed, the mentally retarded, the speech impaired, and the physically handicapped (Kvaraceus, 1956; Gowman, 1957; Murphy, Dickstein, & Dripps, 1960; Warren & Turner, 1963; Appell, Williams, & Fishell, 1963; Rickard, Triandis, & Patterson, 1963). Here again, as with the two and three response category, the instrument is weak because it is non-scorable. The ranking procedure uses an ordinal scale instead of the more precise interval scale. Non-parametric statistics can be used, but not parametric. The ordinal scale and non-parametric statistics limit the full use of measures of central tendency; i.e., medians but not means may be computed. Further limitations are imposed because ordinals cannot be added, subtracted, or divided.

Ranking scales, in spite of their apparent weaknesses, have been used to elicit differences in attitude toward various types of disability. Kvaraceus (1956) found that graduate students would rather teach the physically disabled than the blind or the deaf. Murphy, Dickstein, and Dripps (1960) found that education students preferred to teach the physically handicapped rather than the hearing handicapped. However, Appell, Williams, and Fishell (1963) found that teachers, doctors, social workers, and psychologists would rather work with the hearing impaired than with the cerebral palsied; and Warren, Turner, and Brody (1964) found that students preferred teaching the hearing handicapped and sight handicapped to teaching the brain injured. None of the preceding studies reported the levels of significance of the preference differences.

A basic weakness of the non-scorable instruments is their intractability to parametric statistical analysis. Replication of the studies using scorable instruments might provide new information.

Simple Scored Instruments

The second general category of attitude measurement is the simple scored instruments. These differ from the first category, the non-scored instruments, in that an attempt is made to weigh and score responses. In general, the simple scored instruments were intended for specific investigative purposes and directed toward specific rather than general attitudes. In most cases, no data on reliability and validity were published. The data published proved to be inadequate for broad application of the scale as a measure of attitudes.

Steingisser (1954) developed a 100-item, 3-point (agree, disagree, neutral) rating scale to provide a scorable measure of attitudes toward blindness. Statements about blind persons were selected from those on which there was at least 75 percent inter-judge agreement as to whether the statement was favorable or unfavorable toward blindness. No other statistical development or analysis was attempted. Steingisser investigated self concept and acceptance of the blind. Her report stated that individuals with low self concept were found to hold more unfavorable attitudes toward blindness.

Bateman (1962) developed a 50-item, 3-point (yes, unsure, no) rating scale for sighted children to rate activities which blind children would be able to perform. Again no reliability or validity data were reported. Total test scores and percentages of responses in each category were related to the degree of contact with the blind. The results of the study indicated that persons who had more contact with the blind tended to obtain more favorable scores. Counter-balancing Batemen's study and others with like findings (Roeher, 1959; Whitman & Lukoff, 1962; Siller, 1964; Chesler, 1965) were six studies which were able to report no significant relationship in terms of inferential statistics between attitudes and extent of contact (Rusalem, 1950; Cowen, Underberg, & Verrillo, 1958; Baskin & Herman, 1951; Coggin, 1964; Human Resources, 1962; Siller & Chipman, 1965). The studies cited emphasize the equivocality of previous investigation. There may be a need for further investigation of attitudes using more highly developed instruments.

A five-point rating scale was developed by Jensen and Kogan (1962) to measure the tendency of parents to overestimate the future capacity of their cerebral palsied children in achieving certain skills. The basis for comparison was staff ratings of a child's future skill potential. Although Jensen and Kogan's scale was scorable, the criterion of staff ratings was viewed by Barclay and Vaught (1964) as too variable and subjective for use as an adequate predictor of future potential.

The improvement of the simple scored instruments over the non-scored instruments was primarily due to more adequate measurement of responses, and scoring techniques which allowed better discrimination among respondents on the basis of total response. Total response, rather than item response, became meaningful with the advance from non-scorable instruments to the simple scored instruments. The inadequacy of the simple scored instrument is due to lack of an equal interval unit of measurement.

Attitude Scales

The third general category of attitude measurement is the attitude scale. This group differs from the simple scale category in its more scientific approach to measurement. The development of attitude scales achieves interval measurement from equal appearing intervals along a continuum. Equal interval measurement made possible the application of more sophisticated techniques of inferential statistics such as analysis of variance and factor analysis. The techniques of interval measurement, paired comparisons, and summated ratings led to the development of psychometrically sophisticated overall attitude measures which could be standardized for use in a variety of studies. Following is a brief review of the development of attitude scales from which evolved the instrument used in the present study.

The first and simplest attitude scale was the Bogardus Social Distance Scale originally published in 1925. In 1929, Thurstone described the method of paired comparisons and the method of equal appearing intervals for scaling and scoring attitude items. In the early 1930's the Likert technique of summated ratings was developed (Likert, 1932). Recently complex and specialized statistical techniques for attitude measurement have been published (Yuker, et al., 1966). The

attitude scale used in the present study is a refinement of the Bogardus
Scale with the addition of Thurstone's paired comparison technique and
Likert-like summated ratings.

The ATDP was first reported at the 1959 American Psychological
Association meeting and published in 1960 (Yuker, Block, & Campbell,
1960). At about the same time, Roeher (1959) developed a 22-item, 5-
point Likert scale of attitudes toward the physically disabled similar
to the ATDP. In 1961, Szuhay developed the Adult Attitude Toward the
Physically Disabled Scale. All of these attitude scales appear to be
further refinements of the Thurstone and Likert techniques for scaling
and scoring.

The ATDP has relatively high reliability and well documented
validity. The ATDP provides a scaled measure of attitudes at six different stages along a positive-negative continuum from: +3 I Agree Very
Much to -3 I Disagree Very Much. Norms have been developed for the
scoring procedure. The instrument permits inferential statistical
analysis and parametric measurement. It is short, easy to administer,
simple to score, and not difficult to interpret. It is suitable for
investigating attitudes toward the disabled in general as well as exploring other variables effecting attitudes. The ATDP was the instrument of choice for the purposes of this experiment and is shown in the
appendix.

The validity of the ATDP was determined with reference to con-
struct validity; i.e., agreement of test scores with other tests, and

14

with reference to predictive validity; i.e., comparison of scores with subsequent measures (American Psychological Association, 1954). ATDP scores were correlated with measures of prejudice and with other variables that have been shown to be correlated with prejudicial attitudes (Yuker, et al., 1960). Variables which appear to be correlated with prejudicial attitudes include personality, behavior, self-concept, and sex.

The "fakeability" of the instrument was tested by having a class of 62 psychology students take the test under different conditions (Yuker, et al., 1960). First the scale was administered under normal conditions. Then the class was instructed to take the test again writing FAKE at the top and simply trying to make a good impression without having to respond honestly.

The mean score for the first administered was 76.1 with a standard deviation of 14.00. The mean score for the second testing was 79.2 with a standard deviation of 16.00. A t test computation of 1.17 was not significant at the .05 level. A correlation between the scores on the two administrations was +.22. The relatively low correlation, and the fact that the difference between means was not statistically significant, suggest that the test is not particularly fakeable. The students were unable to make their responses appropriate to earn higher scores.

Yuker, et al. (1966) showed by a number of studies that the ATDP measures attitudes toward disabled persons. The scale takes only about 15 minutes to administer. There is a simple standard procedure

for giving the test. Interpretation of the results is clear and under-

standable. Parametric statistics may be used in analysis of the data

because the ATDP is based on an equal interval scale. When compared

with other instruments, only the Roeher scale (1959) came close to the

ATDP in terms of suitability for the present study. The ATDP was the

instrument of choice because of its sophisticated design, adaptability

for parametric statistical analysis, simplicity, brevity, reliability,

validity, and appropriateness for the purpose of investigating attitudes

toward disabled persons.

Other Scorable Techniques

The fourth and final category of attitude measuring instru-

ments may be called other scorable techniques. Most of these measures

are unique and highly specialized. One of these specialized measures

was Szuhay's (1961) Children's Picture Sociometric Scale. It was

developed solely to study the relationship of mothers and their children

toward disabled children and Negroes.

Another unique measure, assumed to reflect social distance,

was devised by Kramer (1965). $\underline{Ss}$ were asked to make distance judgements

of a number of pictures, some of which were of disabled persons. Result-

ing differences between distance settings for pictures of disabled and

non-disabled persons were assumed to reflect feelings of social dis-

tance.

A preponderance of one-shot studies, single disability investigations and limited evidence of reliability and validity is evident in a review of the literature. Attitude measurement was often based on subjective judgement rather than objective criteria.

Summary of Instrument Development

The simplest instruments for assessing attitudes are the unstructured non-scorable questionnaires or interviews. These instruments do not provide measures that permit inferential parametric statistical analysis. The non-scorable structured schedules are an improvement over the unstructured instruments but do not lend themselves to inferential statistical analysis. Ranking procedures are the most sophisticated of the non-scored instruments, but are not suitable for parametric statistical analysis.

Simple scored instruments attempt to weigh and score responses. However, their use has been limited to specific investigative purposes. Data regarding the reliability and validity of simple scored instruments are inadequate for application to measures of attitudes toward disabled persons generally.

Attitude scales are the most sophisticated of the attitude measuring instruments. Some attitude scales have combined interval measurement and summated ratings to achieve applicability of inferential statistical analysis. Validity, reliability, and standardized procedures have been established for some of the more widely used attitude scales.

Other scorable techniques include those highly specialized measuring instruments which have been designed for more or less unique studies found in the literature. These specialized measures are unsuitable for studying attitudes toward disabled persons generally.

For the purpose of the present study, an attitude scale (ATDP) which combines equal interval measurement, paired comparisons, and summated ratings appeared to be the most suitable for measuring attitudes toward disabled persons.

Attitude Studies

Attitude studies may be classified in terms of the relative frequency of occurrence in the literature as indicated by a review of Psychological Abstracts from 1957 through 1967. Studies of attitudes related to ethnic, religious, and cultural groups constitute approximately 80% of the total. Investigations of attitudes toward specific disability groups, such as the blind or the mentally ill make up almost 5% of the studies. But attitude studies concerning the disabled in general constitute less than 1.5% of the total. The need for the present study may be justified in part by the paucity of knowledge relating to attitudes toward the disabled in general and the lack of agreement of results in those few studies which are available (Yuker, et al., 1966).

The report of an investigation by Badt (1957) indicated that students misunderstood the handicapped and were disinclined to be their teachers. The questionnaire method was used to investigate attitudes of two groups of students at the University of Illinois. The students

18

were grouped as education majors and non-education majors. The investigation concerned their attitudes toward exceptional children and toward providing education services.

The education students were just as unwilling to teach special classes as the other respondents were. They showed less acceptance of crippled children than did the non-education students. The non-education students were openly hostile toward mentally retarded and maladjusted children. The education students expressed unfavorable attitudes which were based on concepts of handicapped children as dependent, demanding, and unstable. They wanted these children segregated.

Badt's (1957) study provided the initial stimulus for the present study. It appeared to the investigator that there should be a continuation of attitude studies, using different measuring instruments and investigating different variables, which may substantiate or refute the findings of Badt.

The problems of special education teacher recruitment were explored in a study by Meyers (1964) who investigated college students' desire to teach the mentally retarded. Meyers used a questionnaire to assess the attitudes of college students in two teacher training institutions. He asked students, both male and female, to indicate their preference of ten possible teaching assignments. Teaching the handicapped was one of teaching assignments interspersed with other possible assignments. All of the students were enrolled in a teacher training program. None had begun taking the teaching methods courses which are required in the last half of the junior year and during the senior year. Most of the students were uncommitted to an area of specialization and could, therefore, select any one of the teaching assignments. The results showed that men for the most part did not respond to questions concerning the handicapped. Women responded but were not favorable toward teaching the handicapped. When the students were asked to indicate which of the groups, if any, they would never teach, even if it meant not teaching at all, a high percentage indicated that they would avoid teaching classes of the handicapped (the percentage was not reported). According to Meyers, the study reveals the great difficulty of special education teacher recruitment. The conclusions drawn by the author of this study suggest that those entering the teaching profession do not, for the most part, want to work with the disabled and that a significant number would leave the teaching field rather than teach handicapped children.

Are Meyer's findings true for elementary education majors who are already enrolled in teaching methods courses? Would a different attitude measuring instrument and a different experimental design achieve different results? Can attitudes toward disabled persons be changed by an introductory course in special education? Some tentative answers to these questions are indicated in the results of the present investigation.

Haring, Stern, and Cruickshank (1958) state that the attitudes of the regular classroom teachers with whom exceptional children are to be placed present a vital consideration which has not been explored.

These authors further state that the attitudes which teachers have are

reflected in their behavior, and influence strongly the social growth

of exceptional children. The statements of Haring, Stern, and Cruick-

shank added impetus to the present investigation of attitudes of college

students preparing for teaching careers in special education and elemen-

tary education. If the attitudes of teachers influence the social

growth of children, then we need to know these attitudes prior to the

time teachers are faced with exceptional children in their classrooms.

If the attitudes of students preparing to become teachers are unfavor-

able toward handicapped persons, then perhaps a means may be sought to

change the unfavorable attitudes.

Mussen and Barker (1944) devised a rating scale to assess the

opinions of the college students toward the behavior characteristics of

crippled individuals. The ratings included 24 personality characteris-

tics ranging from favorable to unfavorable. Ratings of the college

students regarding their attitudes toward the crippled were generally

unfavorable. A more powerful instrument and a different design might

produce results which would further substantiate the findings of Mussen

and Barker, or indicate a need for reconsideration of the study.

Barker, Wright, and Meyerson (1953), in an exhaustive review

of the literature, summarized the characteristics of the attitudes that

other individuals have toward handicapped persons and the attitudes the

handicapped have toward themselves. The findings were based mainly on

21

studies of attitudes toward special groups such as the blind or the deaf. The summary indicates that the attitudes of other individuals toward handicapped persons are mostly unfavorable, as are the attitudes of the handicapped toward themselves.

Johnson (1950) used a sociometric technique to study the social position of mentally retarded children in the regular grades. Children from 25 regular classrooms, each having one or more mentally retarded children, were selected. The author found that the mentally retarded children were rejected by their classmates significantly more times than normal children. He also found that rejection scores decreased steadily as intelligence increased.

In a study by Grebler (1952), using the case study approach with parents of mentally retarded children, it was found that nine out of eleven parents studied felt either ambivalent or rejecting toward their retarded child. The parents were generally extra-punitive in dealing with blame; i.e., they were able to direct their hostile and aggressive attitudes toward others such as teachers, other professionals and the other parent.

Haring, Stern, and Cruickshank (1958) concluded that research was grossly limited with regard to attitudes toward handicapped persons. However, they pointed out that it was obvious from the few existing studies that handicapped individuals are accepted to a lesser degree than those persons who are not handicapped. Although very little research had been conducted on the attitudes of teachers, Haring, et al. (1958)

22

assumed that teachers, too, felt less accepting toward the handicapped than toward typical children.

Summary and Conclusions

The concept of attitude has played a major role in the history of education, psychology, and sociology. During the past sixty years attitude measuring instruments have developed from simple unstructured non-scorable devices to their present level of sophistication. Interval measurement techniques, the method of paired comparisons, and the summated ratings procedure were combined during the late 1950's. The result was the modern attitude scale exemplified in the instruments developed by Yuker, et al. (1960) and by Roeher (1959).

Badt (1957) was one of the first investigators to show that the attitudes of college students, both education majors and non-education majors, were unfavorable toward handicapped children. She stressed the need for a means of changing these unfavorable attitudes.

The problems of special education teacher recruitment were explored by Meyers (1964) who found a general unwillingness among college students to teach handicapped children. The study revealed the difficulty of special education teacher recruitment.

The need for exploring the attitudes of those who are regular classroom teachers, or those preparing to become teachers, was pointed out by Haring, Stern, and Cruickshank (1958). The authors assumed that the attitudes of teachers toward exceptional children in their regular

23

classrooms are reflected in their behavior toward the children and influences strongly the social growth of the exceptional children.

Mussen and Barker (1944) rated the attitudes of college students toward crippled individuals as generally unfavorable. A review of the literature of attitudes toward the handicapped by Barker, et al. (1953) was mostly unfavorable. Johnson (1950) found mentally retarded children rejected by their classmates. A study by Grebler (1952) found parents ambivalent or rejecting toward their retarded child.

Questions raised by the reviews of previous studies include: What are the attitudes of various groups toward disabled persons? Can these attitudes be changed? Is new experimental evidence needed to substantiate or refute previous studies? What variables are significant in attitude assessment? These questions are explored in relation to the present study in Chapter VI.

IV. METHOD

Overview

University students in engineering, elementary education, business, special education, and mathematics classes were given an attitude scale in a pretest-posttest paradigm. Ten classes participated in the study. Three of the classes were exposed to an introductory course in special education. The other seven classes were included to determine if differences existed among groups on the basis of course orientation, sex, age, and grade level.

Subjects

Two hundred eighty subjects, 166 females and 114 males, enrolled at Florida State University were selected on the basis of their inclusion in the ten classes which were compared. The ten groups consisted of three special education classes, one mathematics class, two engineering classes, one business class, and three elementary education classes. The groups were drawn from the College of Education, the School of Business, the College of Engineering Science, and the Department of Mathematics. Three special education classes were exposed to the treatment variable, which was the introductory course in special education.

Instrument

The Attitude Toward Disabled Persons Scale (ATDP), Yuker, Block and Campbell, 1960, was selected as the instrument to be used in this study. Factors relating to the selection of the ATDP have been discussed in the review of the literature (p. 18). The validity and reliability of this scale have been established by Yuker, et al. (1966). They found the reliability to be +.71 (test-retest) and +.83 (split half.). The norms that have been established by the Human Resources Center using the ATDP will be compared with the results of the present study.

Experimental Design

For the purpose of this study the investigator selected an experimental design referred to by Campbell and Stanley (1966) as the Nonequivalent Control Group Design. The design involved experimental groups and control (or comparison) groups in a pretest-posttest paradigm. The comparison group and the experimental group did not have pre-experimental sampling equivalence. Instead, the groups constituted naturally assembled collectives (classes) as similar as availability permitted, but not so similar that one could dispense with the pretest.

A model of the design may be conceptualized as follows: X represents the exposure of a group to an experimental variable, the effects of which are to be measured and 0 will refer to the process of measurement. The X's and 0's in a given row are applied to specific persons. The left-ro-right dimension indicates the time sequence, and X's and 0's vertical to one another are simultaneous. Another diagramatic convention is that parallel rows separated by a dashed line represent comparison groups not equated by random assignment.

```
0               X           0
---------------------------------
0                           0
```

The exposure of the group to the experimental variable is
assumed to be random. That is, the assignment of the treatment to each
individual in the group may be considered as fortuitous.

The Nonequivalent Control Group Design may be regarded as
controlling the main effects of history, maturation, testing, and instrumentation, in that the differences for the experimental group between
pretest and posttest (if greater than that for the comparison group)
cannot be explained by main effects of variables that affect both the
experimental and control groups.

Lindquist's (1953, pp. 172-189) rationale for the analysis of
covariance indicated that test was suitable for the statistical treatment
of this investigation. Essentially, the class means were used as the
basic observations, and treatment effects were tested against variations
in these means. The analysis of covariance used pretest means as the
covariate. Analysis of variance and multiple range tests were applied to
the data.

All experimental designs have strengths and weaknesses. There
are extraneous variables such as history, maturation, testing, and instrumentation which jeopardize internal validity unless controlled in
the experimental design. Internal validity refers to the basic minimum
without which an experiment is uninterpretable: Does the experimental
treatment make a difference in this specific experimental instance?

External validity relates to generalizability: To what populations or situations can this effect be generalized? Factors jeopardizing validity or representativeness include: The interactive effect of testing, the interactive effect of selection biases and the reactive effects of experimental reactives. The selection of the Nonequivalent Control Group Design was based on the ability of this particular model to control these extraneous variables. However, it must be noted that some weaknesses do exist. The particular experimental design selected for this research study, while strong in control of history, maturation, testing, instrumentation, selection, and attrition, is weak in controlling interaction of selection and interaction of testing. These factors are noted and considered in the analysis and interpretation of the results of this study.

Procedure

The criterion measure, ATDP, was administered to students in their college classroom groups. The ATDP was administered on the first day of classes at the beginning of an academic quarter (pretest) and again at the end of the quarter (posttest). A standardized administration procedure was used as prescribed by Yuker, et al. (1966). Responses were scored according to the method recommended by Yuker, et al. (1966).

The first hypothesis, comparing the mean of the ATDP pretest scores with the mean ATDP posttest scores following exposure to an introductory course in special education, was tested by multiple analysis t tests and by an analysis of variance.

The second hypothesis which compares the mean of the ATDP pretest scores of groups choosing to take an introductory course in special education with the means of the ATDP pretest scores of other groups in elementary education, mathematics, business, and engineering was tested. A multiple comparison technique, namely, the Duncan Multiple Range Test and an analysis of variance were used for the purpose of testing hypothesis two.

The third hypothesis, comparing the mean of ATDP pretest scores of groups choosing people oriented courses with the mean of the ATDP pretest scores of groups choosing more technically oriented courses, was tested by Duncan Multiple Range Tests and by analysis of variance. People oriented courses refers to special education and elementary education while technically oriented courses refers to engineering, business, and mathematics.

The fourth hypothesis, comparing the mean of the ATDP pretest scores of each group not exposed to the special education course with the mean of the group's ATDP posttest scores, was tested. Multiple analysis t tests and analysis of variance were used to determine the significance of differences.

The fifth hypothesis, comparing the mean of the combined ATDP pretest scores of all females from all eight groups with the mean of the combined ATDP pretest scores of all males, was tested. The Duncan Multiple Range Test and the analysis of variance were applied to the data.

The sixth hypothesis, comparing the means of the combined ATDP pretest scores of all groups at each age level, was tested. The statistical procedures of choice were the analysis of variance and the Duncan Multiple Range Test.

The seventh hypothesis, comparing the means of the combined ATDP pretest scores of all sophomores, all juniors, all seniors, and all graduate students, was tested. The significance of differences was tested by analysis of variance and the Duncan Multiple Range Test.

Finally, an analysis of covariance was applied to the data to assess the significance of variations among means. Results were compared with normative data supplied by the Human Resources Center.

V.   RESULTS

Hypothesis 1.

The means of the ATDP pretest scores of groups choosing to take an introductory course in special education were not significantly different at the .05 Alpha level of confidence from the mean of their posttest scores following exposure to an introductory course in special education.   However, the results leave the hypothesis open to question.

The statistical analysis of the pretest means showed no significant difference at the .05 Alpha level of confidence among the three groups.

Group 1 showed a slight increase in the posttest mean which was not statistically significant at the .05 Alpha level of confidence. Higher scores on the ATDP indicate a more favorable attitude.   Group 2, on the other hand, showed a slight drop in the posttest mean which also was not statistically significant.   Group 3 showed a statistically significant difference at the .01 Alpha level of confidence.   The Group 3 change was in a negative, or unfavorable, direction.

The results of the Multiple Analysis t test performed upon the means of the three groups are shown in Table 1.   The weighted ATDP scores were used.

31

TABLE 1

MULTIPLE ANALYSIS t TESTS AND F RATIOS
OF PRE AND POSTTEST MEANS FOR 3 TREATMENT GROUPS

Group	Variable		Sample Mean	t Value	df	F Ratio	df
1) 305-1	1) Pre		114-9412	.759	32	1.603	(16, 16)
	2) Post		120-5294				
2) 305-2	1) Pre		114.5333	-1.999	28	1.380	(14, 14)
	2) Post		103,4000				
3) HAS-305	1) Pre		116.5714	-4.600	138	6.818	(69, 69)
	2) Post		84,5286				

Hypothesis 2.

The means of the ATDP pretest scores of groups choosing to take
an introductory course in special education (Groups 1, 2, and 3) were not
significantly different at the .05 Alpha level of confidence from the
means of the ATDP pretest scores of other groups in engineering (Groups 7
and 8), business (Group 9), mathematics (Group 10), and elementary education (Groups 4, 5, and 6). The hypothesis of equal pretest means among
the ten groups cannot be rejected.

The results of the Analysis of Variance and the Duncan Multiple
Range Test performed upon the pretest means of all ten groups are shown

in Table 2 and 3.

TABLE 2

ANALYSIS OF VARIANCE AMONG PRETEST MEANS
OF ALL TEN GROUPS

	Sum of Squares	df	Mean Square	F Ratio
Between Groups	3398.6094	9	377.6233	1.0080
Within Groups	101145.2620	270	374.6121	
TOTAL	104543.8714	279		

The F ratio was not statistically significant at the .05 Alpha level of confidence. All ten groups formed one homogeneous set. No pair of groups differed by more than the shortest statistically significant range for a subset of that size.

TABLE 3

PRETEST MEANS OF ALL CLASSES
IN RANKED ORDER

Rank	Class	Mean	Number of Replications	Group
1	431-2	108.23	22	5
2	495-69	110.46	37	8
3	MAN352	111.88	26	9
4	431-1	111.94	17	4
5	495-68	113.61	28	7
6	305-2	114.58	15	2
7	305-1	114.94	17	1
8	HAS305	116.57	70	3
9	EED432	117.61	23	6
10	MAT426	121.12	25	10

Hypothesis 3.

The means of the ATDP pretest scores of groups choosing people oriented courses (special education and elementary education) will be equal to the means of the ATDP pretest scores of groups choosing more technically oriented courses (engineering, business, and mathematics). The null hypothesis (3) as stated above cannot be rejected on the basis

34

of the statistical analysis which showed no significant differences at
the .05 Alpha level of confidence among means of the ten groups.

The results of Analysis of Variance and the Duncan Multiple
Range Tests performed upon the means of the groups are shown in Table 4
and 5. The results indicate that there are no statistically significant
differences among the means of the groups regardless of orientation.

TABLE 4

ANALYSIS OF VARIANCE OF PRETEST MEANS
OF TEN GROUPS

	Sum of Squares	df	Mean Square	F Ratio
Between Groups	3398.6094	9	377.6233	1.0080
Within Groups	101145.2620	270	374.6121	
TOTAL	104543.8714	279		

TABLE 5

PRETEST MEANS, STANDARD DEVIATIONS, AND RANK ORDER
OF ALL TEN CLASSES

Group	Class	Mean	Standard Deviation	Number of Replications	Rank
1	305-1	114.94	18.8264	17	5
2	305-2	114.53	16.4224	15	6
3	HAS305	116.57	20.8435	70	8
4	431-1	111.94	21.6289	17	4
5	431-2	108.23	19.8732	22	1
6	EED432	117.61	18.7489	23	9
7	495-68	113.61	16.6719	28	5
8	495-69	110.46	17.3695	37	2
9	MAN352	111.88	21.6912	26	3
10	MAT426	121.12	18.3492	25	10

The results of the Duncan Multiple Range Test showed one homogeneous set made up of subsets of elements, no pair of which differed by more than the shortest significant range for a subset of that size.

Hypothesis 4.

The mean of the ATDP pretest scores of each group not exposed

36

to the introductory course in special education will be equal to the mean of the group's ATDP posttest scores. The null hypothesis as stated in the preceding sentence cannot be rejected on the basis of the statistical analysis.

Only one group showed a statistically significant difference at the .05 Alpha level of confidence. The group that differed significantly was 495-69, a class of engineering students who did not want to take the posttest because they had expected to be dismissed early. Some of this group verbalized their hostility and some refused to take the test, others simply checked the first response on all thirty items of the instrument. It appears that the posttest is invalid in view of the expressed resentment toward the posttest. The testing situation was peculiar to the one group. Note the non-significant difference in the other class of engineering students, 495-68, Table 6.

The results of the multiple analysis t tests and analysis of variance performed on the means of the groups are shown in Table 6 and 7.

TABLE 6*

CLASS MEANS, STANDARD DEVIATIONS, AND VARIATIONS
ON PRE AND POSTTESTS OF COMPARISON GROUPS

Group and Class	Variable		Sample Size	Sample Mean	Sample Variance	Sample Standard Deviation
4) 431-1	1)	Pre	17	111.9412	467.8088	21.6289
	2)	Post		113.4118	528.8824	22.9974
5) 431-2	1)	Pre	22	108.2274	394.9459	19.8732
	2)	Post		113.9091	308.4675	17.5632
6) EED432	1)	Pre	23	117.6087	351.5217	18.7489
	2)	Post		119.3043	256.0395	16.0012
7) 495-68	1)	Pre	28	113.6071	277.9511	16.6719
	2)	Post		111.7500	451.9722	21.2596
8) 495-69	1)	Pre	37	110.4595	301.6697	17.3695
	2)	Post		71.3784	2850.8529	53.3934
9) MAN352	1)	Pre	26	111.8846	470.5062	21.6912
	2)	Post		116.6154	388.4862	19.7101
10) MAT426	1)	Pre	25	121.1200	336.6933	18.3492
	2)	Post		121.4000	468.0833	21.6352

*Presents post hoc descriptive data.

TABLE 7*

RESULTS OF MULTIPLE ANALYSIS t TESTS AND ANALYSIS OF VARIANCE
WITH t VALUES AND F RATIOS OF COMPARISON GROUP MEANS

Select No.	(Base) Group	Variable	(Compare to Base) Group	Variable	t Value	df	F Ratio of Variances	df (N1-1, N2-1)	
4.1	4) 431-1	1) Pre	4) 431-1	2) Post	.192	32	1.131	(16,	16)
5.1	5) 431-2	1) Pre	5) 431-2	2) Post	1.005	42	1.280	(21,	21)
6.1	6) EED432	1) Pre	6) EED432	2) Post	.330	44	1.373	(22,	22)
7.1	7) 495-68	1) Pre	7) 495-68	2) Post	-.364	54	1.626	(27,	27)
8.1	8) 495-69	1) Pre	8) 495-69	2) Post	4.234	72	9.449	(36,	36)
9.1	9) MAN352	1) Pre	9) MAN352	2) Post	.823	50	1.211	(25,	25)
10.1	10) MAT426	1) Pre	10 MAT426	2) Post	.049	48	1.390	(24,	24)

*Presents post hoc descriptive data.

Hypothesis 5.

The mean of the combined ATDP pretest scores of all females from
all ten groups did not show a statistically significant difference at the
.05 Alpha level of confidence when compared with the mean of the combined
ATDP pretest scores of all males from all groups.

The hypothesis, that the mean of the scores of all males and females will be equal, cannot be rejected on the basis of the statistical

analysis of the groups.

The results of the analysis of variance are shown in Table 8. Table 9 shows means, standard deviations, and rank order of males and females.

TABLE 8

ANALYSIS OF VARIANCE BETWEEN PRETEST MEANS
OF MALES AND FEMALES

	Sum of Squares	df	Mean Square	F Ratio
Between Groups	1144.7892	1	1144.7892	3.0770
Within Groups	103399.0822	278	371.9391	
TOTAL	104543.8714	279		

TABLE 9

PRETEST MEANS OF MALES AND FEMALES IN RANK ORDER

Group	Sex	Mean	Standard Deviation	Number of Replications	Rank
1	Male	111.94	17.8520	114	1
2	Female	116.05	20.2090	116	2

40

The multiple range test indicated that there was one homogeneous set made up of two subsets which do not differ by more than the shortest statistically significant range for a subset of that size.

The F ratio was not statistically significant at the .05 Alpha level of confidence; therefore, the difference between males and females was not statistically significant.

Hypothesis 6.

The mean of the combined ATDP pretest scores of all groups at each age level will be equal. The null hypothesis cannot be rejected on the basis of the present statistical analysis. The five age groups (19 years, 20 years, 21 years, 22 years, and 23 years and above) did not show a statistically significant difference at the .05 Alpha level of confidence when the analysis of variance was applied to the data.

The results of the analysis of variance are shown in Table 10.

TABLE 10

ANALYSIS OF VARIANCE OF PRETEST MEANS OF FIVE AGE GROUPS

	Sum of Squares	df	Mean Square	F Ratio
Between Groups	2151.6789	4	537.9197	1.4447
Within Groups	102392.1925	275	372.3352	
TOTAL	104543.8714	279		

The results of the Duncan Multiple Range Test are shown in Table 11.

TABLE 11*

FIVE AGE GROUPS WITH MEANS AND RANK

Group	Age	Mean	Standard Deviation	Number of Replications	Rank
1	19	113.19	25.6875	27	2
2	20	113.94	20.2115	68	3
3	21	115.98	19.2083	120	4
4	22	107.29	14.9269	31	1
5	23	117.00	14.8487	34	5

*Presents post hoc descriptive data.

The hypothesis cannot be rejected although the 22-year-old group mean deviates significantly from the average of the other four groups. A possible explanation of this phenomenon is suggested in Chapter VI.

Hypothesis 7.

The means of the combined ATDP pretest scores of all groups at each grade level (sophmores, juniors, seniors, and graduate students) will be equal.

Multiple range tests and an analysis of variance indicated that there are no statistically significant differences at the .05 Alpha level of confidence among the four grade levels which were tested. Therefore, hypothesis seven cannot be rejected on the basis of the present study.

The results of the analysis of variance and multiple range tests performed upon the means of the four groups are shown in Table 12 and 13.

TABLE 12

ANALYSIS OF VARIANCE OF PRETEST MEANS
AT FOUR GRADE LEVELS

	Sum of Squares	df	Mean Square	F Ratio
Between Groups	1502.5975	3	500.8658	1.3416
Within Groups	103041.2739	276	373.3379	
TOTAL	104543.8714	279		

43

TABLE 13

MULTIPLE RANGE TESTS OF PRETEST MEANS
IN RANK ORDER

Group	Grade Level	Mean	Standard Deviation	Number of Replications	Rank
1	Soph.	109.55	25.4553	22	1
2	Jr.	111.94	20.6197	80	2
3	Sr.	116.05	17.9422	161	3
4	Grad.	116.29	16.4650	17	4

There is one homogeneous set made up of subsets of elements, no pair of which differ more than the shortest significant range for a subset of that size.

The general linear hypothesis and analysis of covariance were used for a final analysis of differences. The pretest means were used as the covariate and the effects of treatment, age, and group interaction were tested against variations in the means. The one treatment group difference, and the age by group interaction were assessed. The F's were respectively .31936, .79403, and 1.43693. None were statistically significant.

A comparison was made with the norms established by the Human Resources Center for means and standard deviations. There were no statistically significant differences between the Human Resources Normative Data on means and standard deviations and those resulting from the present study.

44

VI. DISCUSSION

The findings of the present study appear to indicate that exposure to a course of study which deals with handicapping conditions,
and which might presumably create better understanding and acceptance
of the handicapped, does not change attitudes and may even result in a
negative change of attitude more unfavorable to handicapped persons than
was the attitude prior to taking the course. These findings of non-
significant differences must, however, be confined to college students
in a southeastern state university who have completed the freshman year.

Three groups took the treatment course; and one group taught
by several instructors changed significantly in a negative and unfavorable direction. A second group showed a slight non-significant negative
change, and the third group showed a slight, but not significantly favorable, change. The experimenter talked with a sample of students from the
group that changed significantly. There was no evidence of hostility or
negative reactions to the testing situation. The students reported, however, that there seemed to be some confusion which resulted from differences of positions or opinions among the various professors who taught
the course.

The present results substantiate some previous studies of
attitudes toward the disabled in terms of changes resulting from courses
of study related to disability (Dixon, 1967; Costin & Kerr, 1962; Cohen &
Struening, 1959). Dixon (1967) found evidence that changes in attitudes

are more closely related to the teacher's position than to course materials related to disability. The effects of an abnormal psychology course in college students' attitudes toward mental illness were shown to be negative (Costin & Kerr, 1962). However, more favorable attitudes were shown to have resulted from an in-service training program for ward personnel in a larger mental hospital (Cohen & Struening, 1959).

An unexpected result of the study was the posttest reaction of one group of engineering students. The engineering class changed significantly and dramatically in an unfavorable direction. The experimenter learned that the group had expected to be dismissed early. The posttest delayed their dismissal and seemed to some like an examination. Some students in the group expressed hostility and resentment. Two students refused to take the posttest and three tests had to be thrown out because the students had distorted the answer sheet. The markedly unfavorable posttest result may indicate an unfavorable attitude toward the testing situation rather than toward the disabled. However, the hostile reaction was peculiar to this group alone and was not evident in any of the other testing situations.

The findings of the present study concur with those of Badt (1957) indicating that students majoring in education are no more favorable toward the handicapped than are non-education majors. However, the findings of Meyers (1964), which indicate that special education teacher recruitment is especially difficult because of unfavorable attitudes toward the handicapped by education majors, is not borne out by the

46

present study since there was no significant difference between those who chose elementary education and those who chose special education.

The study by Mussen and Barker (1944) appears to reflect a more unfavorable attitude toward the handicapped by college students than that which resulted from the present study. The methods of investigation were so different, however, that the comparison is inductive rather than statistical. It may be that the Mussen and Barker findings reflected attitudes toward the disabled which existed 24 years ago but have changed since that time.

Although the evidence is equivocal, Yuker, et al. (1966) found a preponderance of studies indicating that the attitudes of females toward the disabled were more favorable than that of males. These findings were not borne out by the present results which found no significant difference between males and females in attitudes toward the disabled.

The difference reported on page 38 for the 22-year-olds is post hoc and admittedly speculative. The ad hoc F test revealed no significant differences and these data are presented for the enlightenment of the reader.

It must be recalled that the experimental design was said to be weak in controlling interaction of selection and interaction of testing. This weakness may, to some extent, account for the non-significant results.

The results of the present study indicated that (1) an introductory course in special education did not result in an attitude change, (2) the variables of academic course selection, grade level, age, and sex were not significantly related to differences in attitudes toward the disabled and (3) the attitudes of college students were not significantly unfavorable toward the disabled when compared with other normative data.

It appears that attitudes toward the disabled are complexly related to many variables that affect each other in ways that are not yet fully understood.

It is recommended that further research investigate Dixon's (1967) suggestion that changes in attitudes are more closely related to the teacher's position than to course materials related to disability.

VII. SUMMARY

Attitudes toward disabled persons can be measured and analyzed statistically by means of instruments only recently developed. In the present study the ATDP was used to assess the effects of five variables upon attitudes toward disabled persons. The five variables were: an introductory course in special education, course selection, age, grade level, and sex.

Measures of attitudes of 280 college students in ten groups were obtained in a pretest-posttest paradigm. Statistical analysis in the form of Analysis of Variance, Multiple Range Tests, Paired Comparisons, Multiple Analysis t tests, and Analysis of Covariance was applied to the data.

The results indicated that none of the five variables were statistically significant at an .05 Alpha level of confidence. However, one group showed an age difference which may be due to change alone. One of the three treatment groups showed a statistically significant unfavorable change which did not appear to be related to the testing situation but may be related to confusion resulting from differing opinions among the various professors who taught the course. One of the engineering course groups changed significantly as an apparent result of the post-test situation. These changes are speculative and may be due to chance alone since the analysis of covariance indicated that there were no significant differences.

Three major problems were investigated; viz: (1) differences between students choosing people oriented courses (special education and elementary education) and students choosing more technically oriented courses (engineering, mathematics, and business), (2) differences in attitudes based on course selection, and (3) differences resulting from an introductory course in special education. The study indicated that there were no significant differences related to the above named variables nor to grade level, age, or sex among the ten groups tested.

REFERENCES

Allport, G. W. Attitudes. In C. Murchison (Ed.)., A Handbook of
    Social Psychology. Worcester, Mass.: Clark University Press,
    1935. Ch. 17.

American Psychological Association. Technical recommendations for
    psychological tests and diagnostic techniques. Psychological
    Bulletin, 1954, 51 (Supplement).

American Psychological Association. Standards for Educational and
    Psychological Tests and Manuals. Washington, D.C.: by The
    Association, 1966.

Appel, M. J., Williams, C. M., & Fishell, K. N. Interest of
    Professionals in Fields of Exceptionality. Vocational Guidance
    Quarterly, 1963, 12 (1), 43-45.

Badt, Margit. Attitudes of University Students Toward Exceptional
    Children. Exceptional Children, 1957, 23, 286-290.

Barclay, A., & Vaught, G. Maternal Estimates of Future Achievement in
    Cerebral Palsied Children. American Journal of Mental Deficiency,
    1964, 69 (1), 62-65.

Barker, R. G.; Wright, Beatrice; Meyerson, Lee & Gonick, Mollie.
    Adjustment of Physical Handicap and Illness: A Survey of the
    Social Psychology of Physique and Disability. (Rev. ed.) New
    York: Social Science Research Council, 1953. Bulletin 55.

Barton, E. H., Jr., Coladarci, A. P., & Carlson, K. E. The Employ-
    ability and Job-Seeking Behavior of the Physically Handicapped;
    Employer's Views. Archives of Physical Medicine and Rehabilita-
    tion, 1954, 35, 759-764.

Baskin, N., & Herman, R. Attitudes Toward Cerebral Palsy. Cerebral
    Palsy Review, 1951, 12 (7), 4-7.

Bateman, Barbara. Sighted Children's Perceptions of Blind Children's
    Abilities. Exceptional Children, 1962, 29 (1), 42-46.

Blanton, R. L., & Nunnally, J. C. Semantic Habits and Cognitive Style
    Processes in the Deaf. Journal of Abnormal and Social Psychology,
    1964, 68, 397-402.

Bogardus, E. S. Measuring Social Distance. Journal of Applied Sociology,

1925, 9, 299-308.

Campbell, D. T. & Stanley, J. C. Experimental and Quasi-Experimental Designs for Research. Chicago: Rand McNally, 1966.

Chesler, M. A. Ethnocentrism and Attitudes Toward the Physically Disabled. Journal of Personality and Social Psychology, 1965, 2 (6), 877-882.

Coggin, D. L. Relationship of Variables Including Contact, Interests, and Sex to Attitudes Toward the Disabled. Unpublished manuscript, Human Resources Library, 1964.

Cohen, J., & Struening, E. L. Factors Underlying Opinions About Mental Illness in the Personnel of a Larger Mental Hospital. American Psychologist, 1959, 14, 339.

Costin, F., & Kerr, W. D. The Effects of an Abnormal Psychology Course on Students' Attitudes Toward Mental Illness. Journal of Educational Psychology, 1962, 53, 214-418.

Cowen, E. L., Underberg, Rita P., & Verrillo, R. T. The Development and Testing of Attitudes to Blindness Scale. Journal of Social Psychology, 1958, 48, 297-304.

Dixon, C. R. Courses in Psychology and Students' Attitudes Toward Mental Illness. Psychological Reports, 1967, 20, 50.

Garrett, C. W. Quo Vadis: A Pilot Study of Employment Opportunities for the Hearing Impaired. Volta Review, 1964, 66 (9), 669-677.

Gowman, A. G. Attitudes Toward Blindness. In A. G. Gowman, The War Blind in American Social Structure. New York: American Foundation for the Blind, 1957, 22 (7), 2485-2486.

Grebler, Ann Marie. Parental Attitude Toward Mentally Retarded Children. American Journal of Mental Deficiency, 1952, 56, 475-483.

Haring, N. G., Stern, G. G., & Cruickshank, W. M. Attitudes of Educators Toward Exceptional Children. Syracuse, N.Y.: Syracuse University Press, 1958.

Human Resources. Yearly Psycho-Social Research Summary. Albertson, N.Y.: By The Organization, 1962.

Jennings, Mureil. Twice Handicapped. Occupations, 1951, 30 (3), 176-181.

Jensen, G, D., & Kogan, K. L. Parental Estimates of the Future Achievement of Children with Cerebral Palsy. *Journal of Mental Deficiency*, 1962, 6 (1), 56-64.

Johnson, G. O. A Study of the Social Position of Mentally Handicapped Children in the Regular Grades. *American Journal of Mental Deficiency*, 1950, 55, 60-88.

Koehler, M. E. The Personal Problems of the Blind Students in a University. Unpublished master's thesis, University of Minnesota, 1933.

Kramer, E. R. A Social Distance Scale. Unpublished manuscript. Human Resources Library, 1965.

Kvaraceus, W. C. Acceptance-Rejection and Exceptionality. *Exceptional Children*, 1956, 22, 238-331.

Likert, R. A Technique for the Measurement of Attitudes. *Archives of Psychology*, 1932, No. 140.

Lindquist, E. F. *Design and Analysis of Experiments in Psychology and Education.* Boston: Houghton Mifflin, 1953, pp. 172-189.

Maglione, W. G. Attitudes Toward the Handicapped Among Rehabilitation Students and College Undergraduates. Unpublished manuscript. Human Resources Library, 1965.

Meyers, C. E. Realities in Teacher Recruitment. *Mental Retardation*, 1964, 2, 42-46.

Murphy, A. T., Dickstein, Joan, & Dripps, Elaine. Acceptance, Rejection, and the Hearing Handicapped. *Volta Review*, 1960, 62 (5), 208-211.

Murphy, G., Murphy, L. B., & Newcomb, T. M. *Experimental Social Psychology*. New York: Harper, 1937.

Mussen, P. H., & Barker, R. G. Attitudes Toward Cripples. *Journal of Abnormal Social Psychology*. 1944, 39, 351-355.

Reeder, L. G. Cardiac Employment Potential in Urban Society. *Journal of Chronic Diseases*, 1958, 8 (2), 230-243.

Rickard, T. E., Triandis, H. C., & Patterson, C. H. Indices of Employer Prejudice Toward Disabled Applicants. *Journal of Applied Psychology*, 1963, 47, 52-55.

Roeher, G. A. A Study of Certain Public Attitudes Toward the Ortho-
    paedically Disabled. Unpublished doctoral dissertation, New
    York University, 1951.

Rosenberg, M. J., Hovland, C. I., McGuire, W. J., Ableson, R. P., &
    Brehm, J. W. Attitude Organization and Change. New Haven: Yale
    University Press, 1960.

Rusalem, H. The Environmental Supports of Public Attitudes Toward the
    Blind. New Outlook for the Blind, 1950, 44, 277-288.

Sherif, M., & Cantrel, H. The Psychology of Ego-Involvements, Social
    Attitudes and Identifications. New York: John Wiley & Sons, 1947.

Siller, J. Personality Determinants of Reaction to the Physically
    Disabled. American Foundation for the Blind Research Bulletin,
    1964, No. 7, 37-52.

Siller, J., & Chipman, A. Personality Determinants of Reaction to the
    Physically Handicapped: II. Projective Techniques. Unpublished
    manuscript. Human Resources Library, 1965.

Steingisser, Edith. The Influence of Set Upon Attitudes Toward the
    Blind as Related to Self-Concept. Unpublished master's thesis,
    University of New Hampshire, 1954.

Strong, E. K. Change of Interest with Age. Palo Alto, Ca. Stanford
    University Press, 1931.

Szuhay, J. A. The Development of Attitudes Toward the Physically
    Disabled. Unpublished doctoral dissertation, University of Iowa,
    1961.

Thurstone, L. L., & Chave, E. J. The Measurement of Attitude. Chicago:
    University of Chicago Press, 1929.

Thorndike, E. L. The Psychology of Wants, Interests and Attitudes.
    New York: Appleton-Century, 1935.

Warren, Sue A., & Turner, D. R. Attitudes of Professional and Pre-
    professionals Toward Exceptional Children. Salem, Oregon:
    Fairview Home, 1963.

Warren, Sue A., Turner, D. R., & Brody, D. S. Can Education Students'
    Attitudes Toward the Retarded be Changed? Mental Retardation,
    1964, 2 (4), 235-242.

Whitman, M., & Lukoff, I. F. Public Attitudes Toward Blindness. New Outlook for the Blind, 1962, 56 (5), 153-158.

Yuker, H. E., Block, J. R., & Campbell, W. J. A Scale to Measure Attitudes Toward Disabled Persons: Human Resourses Study Number 5. Albertson, N.Y.: Human Resources, 1960.

Yuker, H. E., Block, J. R., & Young, Janet H. The Measurement of Attitudes Toward Disabled Persons. Albertson, N. Y.: Human Resources Center, 1966.

CODE #_____   ATDP SCALE   ANSWER SHEET

Use this answer sheet to indicate how much you agree or disagree with
each of the statements about disabled people on the attached list. Put
an "X" through the appropriate number from +3 to -3 depending on how
you feel in each case.

+3: I AGREE VERY MUCH   -1: I DISAGREE A LITTLE
+2: I AGREE PRETTY MUCH   -2: I DISAGREE PRETTY MUCH
+1: I AGREE A LITTLE   -3: I DISAGREE VERY MUCH

<u>PLEASE ANSWER EVERY ITEM</u>

(1)   -3 -2 -1 +1 +2 +3   (16) -3 -2 -1 +1 +2 +3

(2)   -3 -2 -1 +1 +2 +3   (17) -3 -2 -1 +1 +2 +3

(3)   -3 -2 -1 +1 +2 +3   (18) -3 -2 -1 +1 +2 +3

(4)   -3 -2 -1 +1 +2 +3   (19) -3 -2 -1 +1 +2 +3

(5)   -3 -2 -1 +1 +2 +3   (20) -3 -2 -1 +1 +2 +3

(6)   -3 -2 -1 +1 +2 +3   (21) -3 -2 -1 +1 +2 +3

(7)   -3 -2 -1 +1 +2 +3   (22) -3 -2 -1 +1 +2 +3

(8)   -3 -2 -1 +1 +2 +3   (23) -3 -2 -1 +1 +2 +3

(9)   -3 -2 -1 +1 +2 +3   (24) -3 -2 -1 +1 +2 +3

(10) -3 -2 -1 +1 +2 +3   (25) -3 -2 -1 +1 +2 +3

(11) -3 -2 -1 +1 +2 +3   (26) -3 -2 -1 +1 +2 +3

(12) -3 -2 -1 +1 +2 +3   (27) -3 -2 -1 +1 +2 +3

(13) -3 -2 -1 +1 +2 +3   (28) -3 -2 -1 +1 +2 +3

(14) -3 -2 -1 +1 +2 +3   (29) -3 -2 -1 +1 +2 +3

(15) -3 -2 -1 +1 +2 +3   (30) -3 -2 -1 +1 +2 +3

APPENDIX: *ATDP SCALE

READ EACH STATEMENT AND PUT AN "X" IN THE APPROPRIATE COLUMN ON THE ANSWER SHEET. DO NOT MAKE ANY MARKS ON THE QUESTION SHEETS.

PLEASE ANSWER EVERY QUESTION

---

1. Disabled persons are usually friendly.

2. People who are disabled should not have to pay income taxes.

3. Disabled people are no more emotional than other people.

4. Disabled persons can have a normal social life.

5. Most physically disabled persons have a chip on their shoulder.

6. Disabled workers can be as successful as other workers.

7. Very few disabled persons are ashamed of their disabilities.

8. Most people feel uncomfortable when they associate with disabled people.

9. Disabled people show less enthusiasm than non-disabled people.

10. Disabled people do not become upset any more easily than non-disabled people.

11. Disabled people are often less aggressive than normal people.

12. Most disabled persons get married and have children.

13. Most disabled persons do not worry any more than anyone else.

14. Employers should not be allowed to fire disabled employees.

*Used with permission of Human Resources Center, Albertson, New York

15. Disabled people are not as happy as non-disabled ones.

16. Severely disabled people are harder to get along with than are those with minor disabilities.

17. Most disabled people expect special treatment.

18. Disabled persons should not expect to lead normal lives.

19. Most disabled people tend to get discouraged easily.

20. The worst thing that could happen to a person would be for him to be very severely injured.

21. Disabled children should not have to compete with non-disabled children.

22. Most disabled people do not feel sorry for themselves.

23. Most disabled people prefer to work with other disabled people.

24. Most severely disabled persons are not as ambitious as other people.

25. Disabled persons are not as self-confident as physically normal persons.

26. Most disabled persons don't want more affection and praise than other people.

27. It would be best if a disabled person would marry another disabled person.

28. Most disabled people do not need special attention.

29. Disabled persons want sympathy more than other people.

30. Most physically disabled persons have different personalities than normal persons.

VITA

The writer is a United States citizen by birth. He was graduated from Columbia University in the City of New York and received the Bachelor of Science degree in elementary education. After employment in teaching elementary grades, in business, and rehabilitation counseling, he returned to Columbia University and earned a Master of Science degree in counseling.

The writer was employed, after receiving the M.S. degree, as a rehabilitation counselor for seven years and later as executive director of health agencies from 1953 to 1964. He was also involved in business enterprises including public relations and fund raising.

The writer attended New York University during seven summer sessions and completed the requirements for the doctorate with the exception of the dissertation. In 1964, he enrolled in the leadership training program in mental retardation of Florida State University. He was appointed to the faculty of Florida State University in July, 1966 and since that time has served as coordinator of the Training Program to Prepare Managers of Programs for the Mentally Retarded.

DATE DUE

AP 7 '82	APR 14 82		
AP 26 '82	APR 22 '82		
GAYLORD			PRINTED IN U.S.A